DATE DUE

MAY 1 8 2007	

JUN

1993

SNAKES

SNAKES

the facts and the folklore

Hilda Simon
Illustrated by the author

THE VIKING PRESS   NEW YORK·

First Edition

First published in 1973 by The Viking Press, Inc.
625 Madison Avenue, New York, N.Y. 10022
Published simultaneously in Canada by
The Macmillan Company of Canada Limited
Library of Congress catalog card number: 73–5154
Printed in U.S.A.
598.1 Reptiles
SBN 670–65315–2
1   2   3   4   5   77   76   75   74   73

Acknowledgments

It is always a pleasure to acknowledge the debt for information owed to the work of others. In this case, Raymond L. Ditmars' *Snakes of the World* tops the list of a number of books, including such well-known publications as *Living Reptiles of the World* by Karl P. Schmidt and Robert F. Inger and *Reptiles* by Angus d'A. Bellairs. I also gratefully recall the help extended to me many years ago by Dr. Herndon G. Dowling, then curator of reptiles at the Bronx Zoological Garden. One of his contributions to my study of reptiles was the gift of a small, agile snake which I kept alive and well in a terrarium for more than four years. In that way I could at first hand observe the behavior of such snakes and gain some of the insights about the care of reptilian pets that I am passing along in this book.

Contents

List of Illustrations

Snakes in Myth, Folklore, and History

Few animals have so persistently engaged and excited the human imagination as have the legless reptiles known as snakes or serpents. Snakes appeared as symbols of both good and evil in the mythologies of some of the earliest civilizations. In ancient Egypt, India, and Greece these reptiles were worshiped as deities or as attendants of gods and were variously credited with supernatural power, wisdom, or deviousness. The fearful fascination with which snakes were regarded probably is associated with the realization that the bite of such a small creature might result in the death of a strong, healthy person only minutes later. Even though a relatively small percentage of snakes is venomous, some of the most deadly species are found in the regions where ancient cultures flourished. Although the giant serpents undoubtedly awed people by their sheer size and strength, it was mainly the poisonous species that accounted for the status of the snake as an object of respect and reverent dread.

Adam and Eve with the serpent in the Garden of Eden (from an engraving by the sixteenth-century German artist Albrecht Dürer).

The snake clan's reputation for treachery can also be traced to experiences with poisonous snakes, as is indicated by a number of biblical references to "vipers" and "adders." In the Western civilizations, however, the concept of the proverbial "perfidious serpent" was based largely, not upon observed fact, but upon the Old Testament story of the serpent in the Garden of Eden that spread throughout the West along with the Christian religion. The treacherous creature that talked Eve into disobeying God and urging Adam to partake of the forbidden fruit became the symbol of evil and perfidy.

Through the centuries many of the greatest artists in the Western world have depicted the scene of Adam's and Eve's downfall. Despite variations governed by the era, nationality, and talent of the individual artists, the scene portrayed in these paintings is basically the same. The tempter usually appears in the form of a snake coiled around the trunk or a limb of the Tree of Knowledge. After centuries of this tradition it seems natural that even people who considered the story only a myth were nevertheless influenced by it in their attitude toward snakes.

But was the "serpent" in the Garden really a snake? It always has been accepted that Eve's tempter appeared in the guise of a serpent. This is all the more remarkable because the story itself makes clear that the tempter could *not* have been a snake but *became* one as a result of its perfidious behavior. We will remember that punishment for disobeying was dealt out not only to Adam and Eve, but also to the tempter. This creature that had been the downfall of the first human beings was condemned to "crawl on its belly and eat dirt" from that day on and forever after. However, if this type of locomotion, which implies an absence of legs, was considered a punishment, then it is obvious that the tempter must have had legs before arousing God's wrath. We therefore have to imagine the "serpent" of this biblical story as some kind of arboreal lizard, a four-legged reptile that lost its legs only in punishment for a treacherous act.

It is interesting to speculate that the ancient Hebrews may have created this legend as a result of their observations and experiences with the poisonous sand vipers of Mesopotamia, which, like all snakes of desert areas, are semiburrowing species. "Treacherous" because of their habit of striking from a half-concealed position under loose sand, the vipers might seem to "eat dirt" when burrowing into the sand to escape the heat. Assuming also that crawling appeared as an especially repulsive and demeaning way of moving about, we have all the ingredients for the story of why the tempter in the Garden was turned into a serpent. Its most fascinating feature is that, by accident or intuition, the ancient Hebrews surmised in this religious myth of thousands of years ago the evolutionary development of snakes that scientists were able to establish only relatively recently. We know today from the fossil record that snakes were in fact preceded by four-legged lizard-like ancestors, and lost their limbs in a long evolutionary process.

Undoubtedly influenced by the story of the expulsion from Eden, Judaeo-Christian cultures regarded snakes with a revulsion that contrasts strongly with the veneration accorded them in many ancient civilizations. Outstanding among these was Egypt, where the asp, a member of the cobra family, was considered sacred. Also known as the Egyptian cobra, though it is not restricted to Egypt, the asp is one of the most widely distributed and most common of all African venomous snakes.

The question of what kind of snake the Egyptian queen Cleopatra used for her suicide after the defeat of her armies by the Romans has been debated for centuries. Topping the list of possibilities were both the asp and the small horned sand viper *Cerastes,* a common Egyptian species. Most scientists today believe that it was the asp, whose nerve poison paralyzes the nerve centers, stops breathing, and kills quickly and relatively painlessly. We know that criminals under sentence of death in ancient Egypt were sometimes given the choice of dying by asp bite as an alternative to a much more unpleasant way of death, and it seems likely that Cleopatra, well aware of that fact, chose the same way out for herself.

The Egyptian cobra is the snake used most often in the performances of North African snake charmers, known as hauis. Though reputedly brutal to his snakes, the haui evidently knows a great deal about the cobra and fearlessly handles even those with poison fangs still intact. During a typical performance the

The Egyptian asp, or cobra.

haui winds a cobra around his neck, puts its head in his mouth, and suddenly presses on a spot directly behind the cobra's head, causing the snake to stretch out to its entire length and become stiff and motionless as if in a trance. Then the haui hurls the rigid snake to the ground, whereupon it beings to move again. This may well be the basis for the biblical tale told in the Second Book of Moses:

> And the Lord spake unto Moses and unto Aaron, saying, When Pharaoh shall speak unto you, saying, Shew a miracle for you: then thou shalt say unto Aaron, Take thy rod, and cast it before Pharaoh, and it shall become a serpent.
> And Moses and Aaron went in unto Pharaoh, and they did so as the Lord had commanded: and Aaron cast down his rod before Pharaoh, and before his servants, and it became a serpent.
> Then Pharaoh also called the wise men and the sorcer-

Headdress of an ancient Egyptian ruler, depicting the sacred asp.

ers: now the magicians of Egypt, they also did in like manner with their enchantments.

For they cast down every man his rod, and they became serpents: but Aaron's rod swallowed up their rods.

The asp, known as *haje* to modern Egyptians, was called *Ara,* "the one who raises himself up," in ancient Egypt. In the Egyptian rulers' headdresses, the portion worn on the forehead showed the cobra in its defensive position—the anterior third of the body raised and the neck expanded to form the so-called hood. Fashioned of gold and often with eyes of precious stones, this ornament was the sign of the ruler's supreme sovereignty. The image of the sacred asp also appears in many other ancient Egyptian works of art and architecture.

Both the Greeks and Romans—who called this cobra *aspis,* from which the English word is derived—took over and embellished many of the Egyptian legends about the snake, thus spreading its fame.

Other poisonous snakes were well known to the Egyptians of that era. The picture of the horned viper *Cerastes cornutus* appears frequently in Egyptian sacred writings because its name, *Fi*, was used as a symbol for the letter "f."

In many Mediterranean cultures venomous snakes—especially vipers—were once thought to have great healing powers. Medicines made from their bodies were greatly sought after as cures for a variety of ills—a practice that survived until a few centuries ago. For an entirely different reason the ancient Greeks considered certain nonvenomous snakes to be sacred to Asclepius, the Greek god of healing, who is often depicted either with an attendant serpent or carrying a wand with a snake coiled around it. Later this symbol was combined with the caduceus, the staff of Hermes, or Mercury, messenger of the gods. The caduceus originally was a thin rod topped by a pair of wings and surrounded by vines, but as Hermes later

Head of the Egyptian falcon-god Horus, displaying the sacred asp.

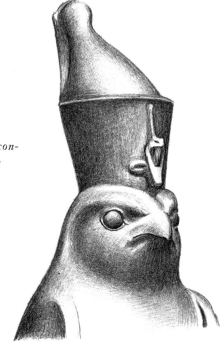

The caduceus, ancient Greek symbol of health, is the insignia of modern physicians.

became identified also with science and medicine, the vines were replaced by snakes coiled around the staff and facing each other at the top. In this form the caduceus is still internationally recognized as the insignia of physicians.

Nobody knows for certain what kind of snake was chosen by the Greeks as the Asclepian symbol of healing; it is, however, possible to make an educated guess that it was a common South European species known as the Aesculapian snake. ("Aesculapius" is the Latinized form of the Greek "Asklepios.") The Aesculapian snake is a member of the rat-snake group and occurs widely in southern Europe and in Asia Minor. In the southernmost portion of its range it may reach a length of five or six feet, but it rarely exceeds three feet in its northernmost range of Austria, Germany, and Switzerland. The fact that only isolated populations of this snake occur north of the Alps and that these are found only in the vicinity of well-known health spas—one such resort in Austria is called *Schlangenbad* (literally, "snake bath")—indicates that the snakes were introduced into these localities by the Romans during their conquests of western Europe. Such evidence suggests that this species was indeed the snake of Asclepius, whose veneration as the god of healing the Romans adopted from the Greeks. The sacred snakes probably were released in the spas to ensure the health-giving power of these resorts.

As for the reason why this particular snake originally was chosen by the Greeks as a symbol of health, the most likely answer lies in its food preferences. Like all members of the rat-snake group, the Aesculapian snake preys on rodents—especially on rats and mice. Also, like most others of its clan, it is not shy and does not mind living in the vicinity of human beings and their settlements, where rats and mice can usually be found. Preferring open, sunny localities, these snakes would naturally have congregated around such spas as the famous baths at Olympia, where prey was easy to find and where stone walls and other structures supplied hiding places. The snakes would have kept such areas free of rats and mice. Although mice were merely a nuisance, rats that came in droves from Asia were dangerous, as they were the main carriers of the fleas that transmit the dreaded bubonic plague. In cities such as Athens or Rome, overcrowding, unsanitary living conditions, and an absence of the rats' natural enemies provided a perfect environment for these rodents, as well as for the transmission of the disease. Presumably the Greeks realized that the presence of large numbers of snakes in a given locality was somehow associated with its relative freedom from plague epidemics, even though they were unable to appreciate the true reason for that correlation. Unaware of the origin of the illness, they could not know that the snakes' seemingly magical powers consisted merely of a voracious appetite for rodents.

An excellent illustration of the firm belief in the ability of these snakes to end epidemics was the order of the Roman

The Aesculapian snake, a member of the rat-snake group, is probably the snake depicted on the caduceus.

consuls Fabius and Brutus during an outbreak of the bubonic plague in Rome. The consuls demanded that snakes be brought from Epidaurus in Greece to an island in the Tiber, where sacrifices were offered to them in an effort to stem the plague.

Greek mythology also has its malevolent snakes, mostly fearful monsters of great strength and ferocity, such as the Hydra, a huge serpent that lived in the marshes of Lerna in the Peloponnesus. It had nine heads and grew two new ones for every one that was cut off. It remained for Hercules to slay that monster. Another huge snake of Greek myth was the Python, after which an entire family of real-life giant snakes was named. This serpent arose from the mud of a legendary flood that killed all human beings with the exception of a single couple. The Python lived in a cave near Mount Parnassus and terrorized the region until the god Apollo slew it; thereafter, the god was called the Pythian Apollo.

Undoubtedly the Greeks were familiar with the giant African python, which may reach a length of some twenty feet, but other attributes of the monster snake were supplied by the lively imagination of the Greek storytellers.

It is worth noting that in west and north European pre-Christian folklore, some of which was incorporated into later myths and legends, snakes frequently play a benevolent role rather than a vicious or treacherous one. Most snakes of Europe are relatively small and nonvenomous; there are no giant snakes or any large deadly poisonous species.

Some references of very ancient origin to "snake kings"—usually white snakes wearing small golden crowns—appear in later west European folk tales. The basis of such myths can probably be found in the rare albino snakes, which would have appeared unusual enough to merit special attention by the storytellers. Albino snakes, by the way, are considered omens of good luck in many countries; in some parts of Asia a white python is believed to ensure the health and good fortune of the lucky finder.

In one old German story, a gleaming white, gold-crowned snake king had become attached to a certain farm where a maid who knew how to treat such royalty set out a dish of milk for him every night. Moved by the kindness of the girl, the snake king was quick to show his gratitude. Snakes appeared in numbers around the farm, which immediately began to prosper as never before. Cows were fat and healthy, gave rich milk, and had many calves; harvests were good; the trees bore record amounts of fruit; and the owner and his family were healthy and happy.

All that, however, was changed when the son of the old farmer took over. The young man, disgusted with the nonsense about the snake king, sternly forbade the maid to waste good milk on a noxious animal and had the snakes around the farm chased and hunted wherever they appeared. Almost immediately the luck of the farm started to change: the cows no longer gave much milk; the calves died; the harvests were meager; the fruit on the trees were full of worms; and sickness struck the young farmer's family. Soon he became poor and unhappy. Realizing that the snake king was avenging himself, the farmer now wanted to make amends. But it was too late— all the snakes had left, never to return.

As in all good folklore, the story is a mixture of facts and lots of fiction. Rodent-hunting snakes that devour rats and mice around farms are an important economic factor even today. Large amounts of feed and grain are lost to rodents wherever the local snake population is decimated. The rest of the story, including the widespread notion that snakes like to drink milk, belongs in the realm of fiction. It does indicate, however, that the feeling of fear and revulsion with which snakes later came to be regarded was not originally the universal attitude of Europeans.

In India and other Asian countries snakes were often exalted as deities or at least associated with gods. Pythons were the sacred symbols of several gods in India. In Kipling's *Jungle Book,* the huge python Kaa was Mowgli's friend and defender. The Indian cobra, a close relative of the Egyptian asp, was regarded with awe and respect mingled with fear, though it was not considered particularly treacherous. The reputation for treachery was reserved for the deadly tic-

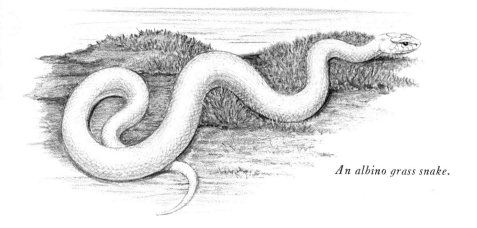

An albino grass snake.

polonga, or Russell's viper, which, according to legend, lives in unrelenting enmity with the cobra.

One folk tale from Ceylon describes how that feud began during a severe drought. A cobra searching for water finally found a well that had not yet run dry, but a child was drinking from it. The cobra quietly waited its turn, drank, and went its way without harming the child. A little while later the cobra met a thirsty tic-polonga. Realizing that the cobra had found water, the tic-polonga begged the cobra to reveal the location of the well. Aware of the tic-polonga's treacherous nature, the cobra hesitated but finally gave in after making the viper promise not to hurt the child. Nevertheless, as soon as the tic-polonga had found the well and quenched its thirst, it bit the child, who died in agony. From that day on, the story claims, the cobra and the tic-polonga have been mortal enemies.

The only factual basis for this story can be found in the characterization of Russell's viper as an especially savage, aggressive snake. Its disposition, along with the high toxicity of its venom and the large size of its fangs, makes it a much more dangerous snake than the cobra.

In China snakes also play an important role in many myths. According to one legend accounting for earthquakes, a giant snake that girds the earth supports it on its coils; when the snake moves, the earth trembles.

Snake worship apparently occurred in prehistoric Mexico, where the snake in the form of a plumed serpent appeared as a symbol of divinity in Toltec and Aztec mythology. Among North American Indian tribes, live snakes played a considerable role in various ceremonial rites. Perhaps the most famous of these rites is the traditional Hopi Snake Dance, performed with rattlesnakes—their venom fangs intact—slung around the dancer's neck or arms. Despite the ever-present dangers in handling the reptiles, it seems that fatal bites were relatively rare, and after the ceremony the rattlesnakes were always released unharmed.

Among the white settlers of North America, the rattlesnake became important as a typically American emblem in the Revolutionary War era. Coiled for a strike, it appeared on several

Three Revolutionary flags with the rattlesnake motif: above left, the first navy jack; above right, the Gadsden flag, hoisted in 1775 on the mainmast of the ship Alfred; *below, the Culpeper flag.*

Revolutionary flags with the legend "Don't Tread on Me," usually with thirteen segments in its rattle, representing the thirteen colonies. One of the earliest of such flags was used by the minutemen of Culpeper County in Virginia. The first navy jack of the fledging American navy, a white flag with red horizontal stripes, displayed a rattlesnake in motion with the familiar legend. This flag was hoisted in 1775 in Philadelphia on the *Alfred*, the flagship of the American navy's first commander.

The choice of the rattlesnake for these flags was based upon several considerations. The lidless eyes of the snake were thought to be brighter than those of any other creature, and thus symbolized vigilance. Though not inclined to attack, the rattlesnake was fearless once aroused, and when it chose to fight it could deliver a deadly bite—which it did only after warning a potential enemy.

Monsters and deities; attendants of gods; symbols of wisdom, health, and power; embodiment of evil and treachery—snakes are all this and more in the folklore of various nations. That these reptiles are still fascinating people today can best be seen from the crowds that are attracted to the reptile houses in every zoological garden. In the chapters that follow, we shall explore the actual life styles of these animals and see what they are like in their natural habitats around the world.

The Evolution and Anatomy
of Snakes

In terms of evolutionary development snakes appeared on the
earth at a relatively late stage; at least that is what the rather
sketchy fossil record of these reptiles leads us to believe. The
earliest known fossils of snakes are from the Cretaceous period about 100 million years ago. By that time the Age of
Dinosaurs was long past, mammals had taken over as the
dominant animal form, and ancient reptiles destined to survive
into modern times—such as crocodiles and turtles—had been
well established for tens of millions of years.

Snakes are thought to have evolved from four-legged,
lizard-like ancestors which were probably more or less aquatic,
coming to the shore mainly to breed and lay their eggs. We
do know that huge, sea-going reptiles called mosasaurs, reaching a length of up to thirty feet, lived in coastal waters more
than 150 million years ago, preying on other aquatic reptiles
as well as on fish. Fossil remains of these mosasaurs have been
found in various parts of the world.

It is assumed that after the mosasaurs came a group of lizard-like reptiles with proportionately long bodies and short legs that were the forerunners of the limbless serpents. This theory is strengthened by the fact that a group of lizards living today show a number of features found in snakes but not in other lizards. These reptiles, the closest living relatives of the snakes, are known as monitors. Most of them are fairly large and heavy and lack the grace of the smaller, slender lizard species. The monitor group includes the giant among all lizards today, aptly named the Komodo dragon, found only on a few small islands in the East Indies. It bears a striking resemblance to the dragons of myths and legends, with its long head and neck, the heavy, thick body and powerful tail, and

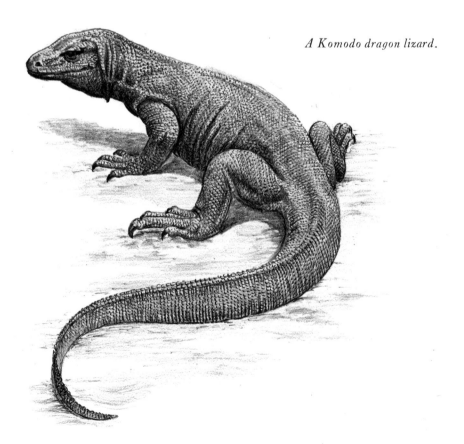

A Komodo dragon lizard.

the strong, sturdy legs with dagger-like claws on the toes. Its slender, forked tongue can be extended far beyond the tip of the snout. One of these giants, which may be three feet high and ten feet long and weigh three hundred pounds, lacks only the breath of fire to be a perfect replica of a mythical dragon.

The Komodo dragon lizard not only looks ugly and dangerous, but actually is a formidable predator with a disposition to match. Although usually a scavenger that feeds on dead or dying animals, it will tackle and kill such large mammals as pigs, deer, and goats if it is very hungry. Its strong teeth and razor-sharp claws can inflict terrible wounds. After the kill, the Komodo dragon rips and tears its prey to pieces, swallowing large chunks without chewing. This habit is unique among lizards but typical of all monitors, some of which may even swallow small prey whole—a characteristic of all snakes, which always swallow their food whole without chewing. Related to this way of eating—and found in both snakes and monitors but not in other lizards—is a solid bony sheath that encases the brain, protecting it from possible damage resulting from pressures of large, solid objects against the roof of the mouth.

Several other anatomical features shared by both snakes and monitors tend to link them to some common ancestor. Neither the snakes nor the monitors can break off portions of their tails voluntarily and later regrow them—an ability that is a hallmark of other lizard groups, including the legless slowworms that superficially look enough like snakes to be frequently mistaken for them. The breakable tail is a handy defensive device permitting many a lizard to escape while its enemy is tackling the wriggling tail tip. Lacking this ability, a monitor or a snake that loses a portion of its tail must live for the rest of its life with a permanently shortened tail. Another feature attesting to the relationship between the two groups is the long, flexible, forked tongue, which is used to pick up the scent of prey with the help of a taste-sensitive organ located in the roof of the mouth. Jacobson's organ, as it is known to zoologists, is most highly developed in snakes, but in monitors it is much more developed than in all other lizard groups.

The closest extant relative of the snakes is a reptile so rare that no specimen has ever been observed in the wild, and nothing at all is known about its living habits. In the entire world there are only six preserved specimens, and it has not been possible to capture one of these animals alive for a zoo. Although it has been assigned the name "earless monitor," it has been placed in a group all by itself because of significant anatomical characteristics that differentiate it from all other lizard groups. Scientists believe that the earless monitor is closely related to the extinct lizards from which snakes are thought to have evolved.

Although we thus know a great deal about snake relatives, both extinct and living, and about the probable line of ancestry, no intermediate forms between these ancestors and actual snakes are known from fossils that would indicate when the first limbless serpents appeared. Remains of a giant snake that lived about 50 million years ago have been found in Egypt; the snake was probably aquatic, and measured some sixty feet in length. A perfect fossil impression from the same period shows a small snake not more than a few feet long and looking very much like the snakes of today.

Despite the lack of fossil evidence of the intermediate evolutionary stages by which four-legged lizards were converted into limbless snakes, zoologists have a very good idea of what these stages were. The forelimbs, along with the supporting bone structure of the shoulder girdle, disappeared first, probably because these bones did not permit the distension of the chest region necessary for reptiles inclined to swallowing their prey whole. After the front legs had been lost, the entire body became more elongated as the animal was compelled to slither and crawl, rather than walk. In the course of these changes,

Fossil, about 50 million years old, of a small snake.

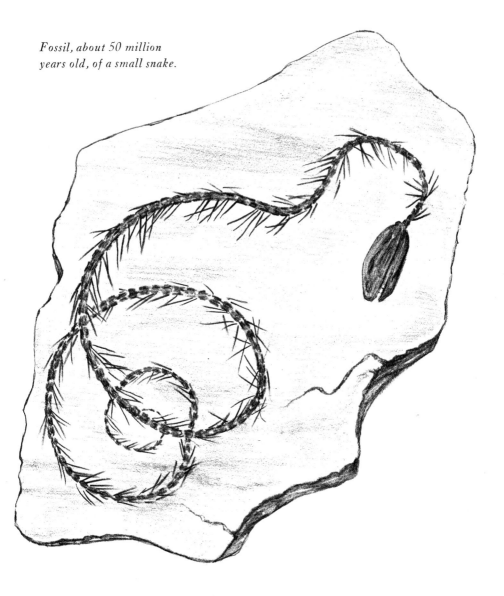

the hind legs could no longer serve any useful purpose and eventually even became obstacles to smooth, undulating movement. Finally, the hind legs also disappeared, along with the supporting pelvic structure. In primitive species of existing snakes, remnants of this bone structure and of hind legs can be found today.

All the ancient snakes were constrictors, killing their prey by suffocating it and then swallowing it whole. The development of venom and the apparatus necessary for delivering it into the bloodstream of the prey came much later. The earliest poisonous snake seems to date from the Pleistocene period, during which large parts of the world, including North America, were covered by glaciers. This snake is thought to have been a veritable monster, measuring sixty feet in length, with fangs as large as those of a tiger. The fossil fang on which this estimate is based was found in the Gran Chaco region of South America.

Along with the lateral undulation as a legless way of locomotion, snakes developed several other anatomical features designed to adapt them better to their mode of living. With the elongated body shape came an increase in the number of ribs—some snakes have as many as four hundred—affording these reptiles great flexibility that permits them to be quite literally tied into knots without harming them. The snake's body also had to become expansible so that large prey could be swallowed whole. In addition, the loosening of the jawbone structure and an increase in the hinge joints in the lower jaw allows the snake to draw its mouth over objects several times the size of its head.

The internal organs also were modified. Both the heart and the lungs became elongated to fit the body shape. All snakes except the most primitive kinds have only one lung, which is

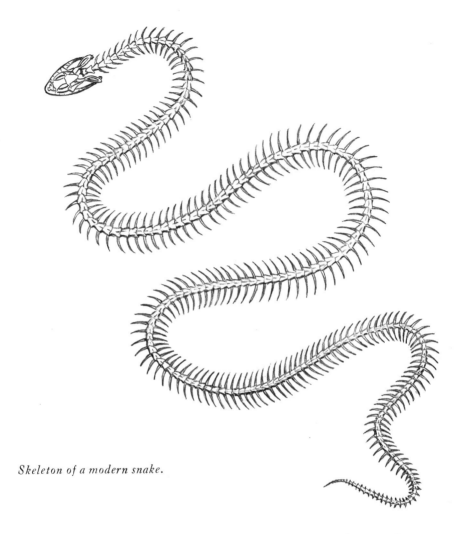

Skeleton of a modern snake.

narrow and very long. In some species, such as certain aquatic snakes, it reaches from the neck to the base of the tail.

The scales on the upper part of the snake's body may be either smooth or rough and keeled, but except in the burrowing species, the scales on the underside are smooth, broad, overlapping plates with sharp edges toward the rear end. This arrangement helps the snake to move forward; muscles attached to the ribs pull and lift these plates, which push against

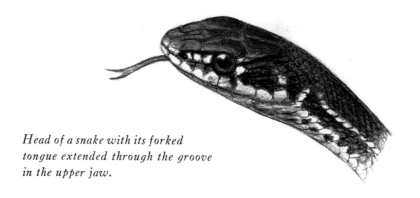

Head of a snake with its forked
tongue extended through the groove
in the upper jaw.

irregularities in the ground or on the bark of trees. Snakes placed on a completely smooth surface find it very difficult to move and make little progress.

The snake's sensory system differs in many aspects from that of other reptiles. As they have no external ears, they cannot hear airborne sounds. It is the snake charmer's movements, not the sounds his flute produces, that make the cobra sway in those famous performances. However, snakes are sensitive to vibrations that can be picked up from the ground.

Snakes generally have good eyesight. In some tree snakes grooves on both sides of the face permit them to have binocular vision. In contrast to lizards, snakes do not have movable eyelids and therefore cannot close their eyes when they sleep. A clear, transparent scale membrane, or "spectacle," protects the eye against injury. Structurally the eyes of snakes also differ considerably from those of lizards. The extent of their color vision, which is very good in lizards, has not yet been fully established.

Despite the fact that snakes have nostrils, their sense of smell, as well as their sense of taste, seems to be located chiefly in their forked tongue, which they flick in and out of the mouth constantly to test the ground and objects in their surroundings. A snake does not have to open its mouth to stick out its tongue, which can be extended and withdrawn through a small groove or notch located at the very tip of the upper jaw.

Though a snake's teeth are delicate and often break off in a struggle with prey, they are soon replaced by new teeth. This is also true of the poison fangs of venomous snakes, which will be discussed in more detail later. All the teeth point backward, a feature that makes it difficult for a snake to disgorge anything—except for liquids and very smooth objects—which it has started to swallow.

The skin of many snakes has a variety of glands, but lacks sweat glands. Snakes thus cannot perspire, which explains why they die from prolonged exposure to hot sun and why desert snakes are usually semiburrowing species. Some snakes have scent glands that leave a trail, enabling the males to track and locate females during the mating season. Snakes molt, or shed their skin, periodically—usually several times a year. Most often the old skin, including the eye membrane, is stripped off in one piece. The colors of a newly molted snake are vivid and bright, its eyes clear.

The anatomical features of reproduction in snakes are similar to those found in lizards. A small majority of snake species are egg-laying, or oviparous, and the others are live-bearing, or viviparous.

Prior to mating, some male snakes become very aggressive, attacking any intruder who invades their territory. The males of some species, especially among vipers, indulge in a form of combat that is mainly a pushing contest with heads reared up, neck to neck. Each male tries to push back its opponent. (See the frontispiece, illustrating territorial combat between two male Russell's vipers.)

Unlike lizards, which locate their mates by vision, male snakes seem to find the females by their sense of smell. A curious courtship habit is the chin-rubbing that many snakes engage in just before mating.

Reproductive habits may vary a good deal even among closely related groups. The European water snake lays eggs, while its American cousins produce live young. Almost all the so-called advanced snakes are viviparous, but this fact does not indicate an evolutionary pattern of development, for many of the primitive snakes also are viviparous, and some of the most advanced species lay eggs. Undoubtedly the live-bearing species have an advantage over the egg-laying kinds because the eggs are incubated in the mother's body instead of being exposed to the hazards of egg-eating enemies and inclement weather. When the young snakes are born, they are fully developed and ready to fend for themselves. This is probably one reason why viviparous snakes, such as the European adder and the North American garter snake, can survive in relatively cold regions.

A snake ready to lay eggs seeks a suitable spot—under flat stones, in moss or rotting vegetation—and then hollows out a shallow depression with her body. Into this "nest" she lays her eggs, which may number from a dozen up to a hundred. The eggs are whitish, oval, and covered by a soft, leathery shell.

Freshly laid snake eggs, with soft shells that change shape as the young snakes develop inside.

Newborn rat snake emerging from the shell, its egg tooth still at the tip of the snout.

A very few snakes guard their nests, but generally the mother leaves as soon as she has laid her eggs, never to return. The heat absorbed by the stones above or generated by rotting vegetation takes over the job of incubating, a process that may last several weeks. The eggs actually grow after they are laid because they absorb moisture from their surroundings. After a while they begin to lose their shape and become lumpy as the young snakes develop inside. When ready to emerge, they punch a hole in the shell with the egg tooth—a sharp point on the snout which soon after falls off—and crawl out into a new and dangerous world. Like its live-born relatives, the young snake is now entirely on its own, with no care, protection, or guidance from its parents.

The world-wide distribution of snakes and their great number and diversity are evidence of their biological success. A loss of limbs might seem to be a regressive, rather than a progressive, adaptation, but snakes actually represent an advanced stage in the evolution of reptiles.

The Giant Snakes

Most people are fascinated by animals of excessive size, and especially by the giant reptiles. Although the largest reptiles that ever lived, the dinosaurs, have been extinct for tens of millions of years, the giant snakes of today are huge enough to be extremely impressive.

All the really large snakes—those attaining a length of twenty feet or more—are found in just two families, the boas and pythons. These two groups are closely related and differ very little in anatomical features and living habits but considerably in their geographical distribution. Most boas occur in the New World, while pythons—with only one exception—are strictly an Old World family found mainly in India and Africa. Another distinction is that pythons lay eggs while boas normally bear live young. The most interesting fact about the reproductive habits of pythons concerns the females' incubation of the eggs. This is most unusual because very few snakes

Female reticulate python incubating her eggs.

—and very few other reptiles, for that matter—pay any attention whatsoever to their offspring, regardless of whether they lay eggs or bear live young. The female python pushes her eggs, of which there may be as many as a hundred at a time, into a pile around which she coils her body, with her head resting on the top. The snake remains in this position throughout the incubation period, which in some cases lasts eighty days, taking time off only for an occasional drink of water. Tests have shown that the body temperature of the brooding female may rise by as much as 12 degrees Fahrenheit above normal—the normal temperature in snakes, as in all so-called cold-blooded animals, being just slightly higher than that of the surrounding atmosphere. It has not yet been established exactly how the snakes manage to raise their temperature during incubation time.

Boas and pythons are among the most primitive of existing snakes. Evidence of this fact can be found in such features as traces of pelvic-bone structure and hind limbs that are externally visible as claws on the underside of the body near the base of the tail. In addition, boas and pythons have paired lungs, while more advanced snakes have only one greatly elongate lung.

All the giant snakes kill their prey by constriction, as do many other nonvenomous snakes belonging to various other groups. It is often assumed that such snakes crush their victims' bones in the process, but this does not happen. Constrictors actually kill their prey by preventing breathing, which stops heart action. In almost all cases, the boa or python strikes at its victim with wide-open, strongly toothed jaws. Once it has secured a hold on the prey, the coils of the snake's body are thrown around the animal and tightened until it is dead by suffocation.

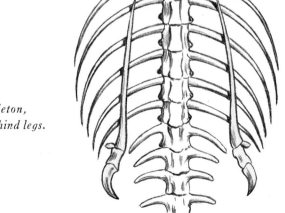

Portion of a boa's skeleton,
showing remnants of hind legs.

Despite many exaggerated reports of the maximum size attained by the various giant snakes, only four species have been found to reach a length of more than twenty feet, and only fairly old specimens actually grow to such a size. The giant among the giant snakes is the regal, or reticulate, python of Burma and southeast Asia. Individuals of this handsomely patterned and colored species are known to have attained a length of thirty-three feet and a weight of more than three hundred pounds. However, specimens over twenty-five feet are rare, and most regal pythons observed or captured measure between fifteen and twenty-two feet. Generally, these big snakes are rather inoffensive in encounters with man and despite their formidable strength try to escape rather than fight. There are many reports of attacks on human beings, but most have been found to be inventions. Among the few authenticated cases of persons being killed by regal pythons was that of a fourteen-year-old boy, who was strangled and eaten by such a snake on an island in the Indian Ocean.

One of the most peculiar habits of the regal python is its preference for living in crowded cities. Years ago these snakes were frequently found in the city and suburbs of Bangkok, especially along the riverbanks, where they were evidently attracted by such tempting and easy prey as various domesticated animals—cats, dogs, pigs, and fowl. The snakes' adaptation to the noise and bustle of man-made environments is all the more surprising in creatures that normally live in dense jungle forests.

The second-largest snake appears to be the anaconda, or water boa, with a reliably reported maximum length of twenty-six feet. Restricted to South America, this olive-and-black-colored giant lives near streams and lakes, where it prowls for the mostly warm-blooded animals upon which it feeds. It

Anaconda killing a captured caiman, a South American alligator.

also attacks half-grown caimans, the South American members of the crocodile group, but it prefers the water fowl and small mammals of the region, especially the capybara, a peculiar water-loving rodent the size of a pig.

Third and fourth in size are the Indian and African pythons, which may reach a length not much less than that of the anaconda. The African python is often called the rock python, which is somewhat confusing because the same name is also used for the Indian species. The African python, which may grow to a length of more than twenty feet, is less heavy-bodied than its Indian relative and therefore does not look as big as an Indian specimen of the same length. (See illustration of the Indian python on page 40.)

All these snakes are similar in their habits, feeding mostly on birds, rodents, and other small mammals. Occasionally, a large individual may attack and overwhelm an animal of considerable size and strength. Thus, a leopard was found in the stomach of an eighteen-foot python. The sharp claws and

An African rock python.

The famous boa constrictor.

teeth of the big cat could not prevail against the strength of the giant reptile, indicating that these large snakes have no effective enemies except for man.

Other members of the two families are generally much smaller, although there is an Australian species that comes close to matching the size of the African python. One of the large New World species is the boa constrictor, a name which many people take to be a synonym for "giant snake." But the boa constrictor, which is found from Mexico throughout much of South America, rarely exceeds a length of ten feet, although fourteen-foot specimens have been known.

The majority of other boas are considerably smaller, although the Cuban boa, which is fast being exterminated, may also attain a length of fourteen feet.

One of the most handsome smaller species is the rainbow boa, a four-foot snake found in Central America and northern South America. Superimposed on a pattern of blackish rings

48   SNAKES

on a rusty-brown background is an iridescence caused by surface structures of the scales, resulting in a play of colors that
gives the snake its popular name. Especially after the periodi-
cal shedding of the old skin, this boa displays a shimmering,
kaleidoscopic range of pure rainbow colors that match the
jewel-like qualities of some birds and butterflies. Although
many snakes of the boa and python families display some iridescence after molting, that of the rainbow boa is by far the
most colorful.

Another very handsome species is the six-foot-long emerald
tree boa of South America, a brilliant green snake with white
or yellowish crossbands on the back. Tree boas, a specialized
group within the family, are found in different parts of the
world, where they have become adapted to a completely arboreal life. Their long teeth—needed for securing a hold on
their mostly feathered prey—triangular, viper-like heads, and
vertical pupils make them look much like poisonous snakes.
With a disposition that matches their looks, most of the tree
boas are savage, aggressive animals that can deliver a painful
bite with their fanglike teeth. The colors of these snakes
range from brown to green, thus providing a good camou-
flage in the trees they inhabit.

A number of small boas have gone to the opposite extreme:
instead of inhabiting the treetops they live mostly underground. These sand boas, as they are known, are burrowers
that spend the greater part of their existence beneath the
surface, where they hunt for lizards and other small subter-
ranean prey. They often, but not always, live in arid regions
bordering on deserts. Their adaptation to a burrowing way
of life include such features as small heads, very small eyes, a
cylindrical, short-tailed body, and small smooth scales. Their
disposition is generally as different from that of the tree boas

A completely arboreal tree boa.

as are their habitats: most of these small boas are gentle and inoffensive and never try to bite.

Several species of sand boas occurring in the western United States are the only representatives of the boa family in North America. The most attractive of these is the two-foot-long

Rosy boa

Rubber boa

Rainbow boa

rosy boa, a pretty, yellowish or pink-hued snake with lateral brown stripes. It occurs in southern California and is frequently found in the chapparral. The rubber boa, whose range is the entire Pacific coast of the United States, from California to the state of Washington, rarely attains a length of even two feet. It is so shy and inoffensive that when captured it rolls itself into a ball and hides its head.

This habit is also typical of certain small pythons, including the attractive, interesting ball python of West Africa. Like the rubber boa, this pleasingly patterned, four-foot-long python is exceptionally gentle and inoffensive and never tries to bite. Its only defense is to coil itself tightly into a perfect sphere about the size and shape of a bowling ball, with its head tucked away somewhere inside. Captured ball pythons often lose their habit of coiling up once they become tame and used to being handled.

An extremely handsome python is the Australian diamond snake, named for the diamond-shaped yellowish markings on a blue-black background. In New Guinea there is a different color phase of this snake, known as the carpet python.

The Australian tree pythons are the counterparts of the New World tree boas. The beautiful green tree python of New Guinea is a perfect match—including the white blotches on a pure leaf-green background—of the handsome emerald boa of South America. Unfortunately, because it is a rare species, it is hardly ever found in zoo collections.

One small group of Australian pythons is unique among pythons in preying exclusively on other snakes, including some of the most deadly poisonous species of the Australian region, such as the tiger and black snakes. Attaining a length of eight feet, these pythons—known as wombas to the Australians—are fearless and efficient hunters of the dangerously venomous

An African ball python, tightly coiled into a ball for defense.

species and for that reason are welcome wherever they appear.

One of the interesting, small African pythons is a three-foot species from the Congo that is a counterpart of the sand boas. It burrows in leaf mold and loose soil, where it finds the small animals on which it feeds. An inoffensive snake that also has the habit of rolling itself into a ball when handled, it is sometimes known as the two-headed snake because its head is so small that it has a superficial resemblance to the blunt tip of its short tail.

Though there are comparatively few species of boas and pythons with a relatively limited geographical distribution, these groups, including the giant species, have successfully adapted themselves to a number of different environments and have survived and flourished until recently. Now, however, many of the large boas and pythons are threatened with extinction, not only because unprincipled people kill them to sell their beautiful skins, but also because their natural habitats are disappearing as a result of the rapid growth of human settlements. Whether they will be able to survive these threats depends largely on the measures taken by concerned people all over the world, people determined to make every effort to preserve such endangered species as these giant members of the reptile class.

Nonvenomous Snakes

Even after excluding the boas and pythons, roughly half of the remaining snake species are harmless, meaning they have either no poison at all or a poison too weak to seriously affect a human being. The largest harmless snakes attain a maximum length of about ten feet, while most species average between two and five feet.

The most primitive among these groups are several families of burrowing snakes. The blind burrowing snakes are generally very small, with the majority reaching a length of only eight inches. Despite their common name, these snakes are not completely blind, but their eyes are minute and often hidden under scales. The giant of the clan is thirty inches long, and the smallest species, often called the flowerpot snake because of its habit of crawling into flowerpots in search of small insects, is a mere five inches when fully grown. This habit of living among the roots of cultivated plants has led to the snake's being accidentally transported all over the world, so that it is now established in many different countries, far removed from its original home in Mexico.

Other burrowing snakes, also generally small species, are noted for their frequently bright and colorful patterns. They may display red, orange, and black hues in a number of striking combinations and are often iridescent. One species is called the sunbeam snake because of the rainbow-like play of pure colors over a dark brownish background.

The more advanced harmless snakes include some of the best-known and common species. Within this group, we find every existing ecological type of snake—terrestrial as well as arboreal forms, and burrowing as well as aquatic species. Some bear live young; most lay eggs that are hatched by the warmth of the sun. In addition there are certain highly specialized types, such as the snake that feeds exclusively on birds' eggs and another that lives on nothing but snails and has special teeth for extracting these mollusks from their shells.

The harmless snakes, grouped in a family known as Colubridae, are for the most part slender species, with a head that is usually not much wider than the neck and with large

A colorful burrowing snake of South America.

Head of a typical nonvenomous snake
seen from side and above.

eyes and round pupils, indicating that the snakes are active during the daytime. The arrangement of the large scales on the head is a good means of identification.

One of the largest groups of common colubrid snakes has chosen a more or less aquatic way of life. These water snakes and their allies are found usually along rivers and lakes, where they feed on frogs, toads, crayfish, tadpoles, and fish. Excellent swimmers, they pursue the fish in the water, which they also seek whenever they are molested or frightened. The American water snakes bear live young, whereas the Old World species, otherwise very similar in habits and habitats, lay eggs. The common European water snake—or grass snake, as it is often called—may lay fifty eggs in a clutch. Many other closely related water snakes occur in India, Africa, and even in Australia, a continent with remarkably few other harmless snakes.

The North American garter snakes are related to the water snakes. Probably the most common of all North American species, garter snakes range farther north than any other snake in the Western Hemisphere. There are a number of different species and subspecies, many of which vary considerably in color and pattern. Generally, the southern species are mainly aquatic, while those in the north have taken up a much more terrestrial way of life. Many garter snakes live mostly on earthworms and vary this diet with small frogs, toads, and, among the aquatic forms, fish. The thin, dainty garter snakes known as ribbon snakes, which live in swampy meadows near rivers and streams, feed predominantly on fish and tadpoles.

The smallest of the water-snake relatives are slender, pretty little brown snakes with secretive habits. They like to hide under bark and stones and feed largely on slugs, worms, and other small, soft-bodied creatures. One of the commonest is DeKay's snake, which occurs widely throughout the eastern United States and may even be found in the parks of large cities. Even more attractive is the red-bellied snake. Both are no thicker than a pencil and average a length of about a foot.

All the water snakes eject a foul-smelling fluid from a gland at the base of the tail when molested, a habit that undoubtedly helps protect them from enemies with sensitive noses.

Common garter snake.

DeKay's snake.

Another of the important groups of familiar terrestrial colubrids are the king snakes and their relatives. In North America many different species and subspecies are represented. The common king snake appears in at least five distinct color forms. In the east it displays a chainlike pattern of yellow on black; in California it has yellowish or white rings or stripes on black; and in the Mississippi Valley it shows a finely speckled white and greenish coloration. The slightly smaller red king, or milk, snake, with its pattern of reddish or brown blotches on a light gray background, is an eastern species, while the beautiful black-red-and-cream-banded Arizona mountain king snake is restricted to a relatively small area in the west. There are nine distinct subspecies of the common king snake and a number of closely related smaller species.

All the king snakes and their relatives in other parts of the world—such as the European smooth snake—have smooth scales and are relatively stout-bodied and slow-moving. They prey upon a variety of small animals, including lizards, frogs, and rodents, although other snakes seem to be on the pre- ferred diet list of the American king snakes. Like most snake- eating snakes, they have extensive immunity to the venom of the poisonous species and will kill and eat rattlesnakes when- ever the opportunity presents itself.

Except for the boas and pythons, some of the largest non- venomous snakes are found in the genus *Elaphe,* commonly

Top to bottom: common king snake, scarlet king snake, California king snake.

known as rat, or chicken, snakes. Members of this group occur in many parts of the world with the exception of Africa. The famous Aesculapian snake is a rat snake, as is the beautiful corn snake, probably the most handsome large snake in North America (see illustration on page 54). All rat snakes, some of which may attain a length of eight feet or more, feed largely on rodents that are injurious to man and his crops. The rat snakes are constrictors, killing their prey exactly as the boas and pythons do, by applying pressure that stops breathing and heart action. They are also good climbers and are often found in trees, where they may stalk birds or rob nests. The popular name "chicken snake" for these reptiles stems from the fact that they steal eggs from hen houses whenever they get a chance and occasionally prey on very young chicks. The yellow rat snakes of the southern United States, for instance, does this regularly as it prowls around chicken coops in search of rats and mice, but it more than pays for the eggs it takes by keeping destructive rodents under control. This snake likes to make its home near human habitations and can frequently be found comfortably curled up in a basket, a pot, or some other such container in barns or garden houses, a habit leading to its other popular name, the yellow house snake.

The largest rat snake is the pilot blacksnake, also known as the black chicken snake or the mountain blacksnake. It has the widest range of all North American rat snakes, occurring in the northeast as well as in Florida and Texas. This snake especially likes to climb and is often found in trees, either stretched out on a large limb, resting after feeding, or prowling around for birds. Like the other rat snakes, it also enjoys eating eggs and robs hen houses whenever it gets the chance. Rat snakes do not break the eggs but swallow them intact and wait for their strong digestive juices to dissolve them, shell and

Black rat snake killing a rat by constriction.

all. One black rat snake was observed waiting in vain for that
to happen: it had swallowed a china egg placed in a hen's nest
and must have been quite surprised when the egg did not dissolve. Finally, it disgorged the unpalatable item.

The Old World rat snakes have very much the same habits,
and are every bit as efficient as their North American counterparts in checking the rodent population. One species ranging

from southeastern Europe to western Asia is the four-lined snake, which is very similar to the American yellow rat snake. Other species occur in various parts of Europe and Asia, but no members of this genus have made their home in Africa.

One of the largest nonvenomous species in North America is the powerful bull snake, found throughout the wheat belt of the United States. Unfortunately, this and other economically useful snakes are often killed by people with no appreciation of their importance. Attaining a length of close to nine feet, the bull snake is distinguished by its ability to produce a loud, threatening hiss when angered or frightened. Its diet is like that of the rat snakes, consisting mainly of rodents and eggs or very young birds, mostly those of ground-breeding species. Its method of eating eggs differs from that employed by the rat snakes. Instead of waiting for the egg to be dissolved by gastric juices, the bull snake presses its throat against the ground after swallowing the egg until the shell breaks.

The western bull and pine snakes are somewhat smaller subspecies of western and eastern North America, respectively. The handsome black-and-white pine snake is found especially in pine barrens. Both have similar habits.

A pine snake, the eastern form of the bull snake.

Blue racer and coachwhip snake.

Differing in habits and appearance from the preceding groups are the racers and whip snakes. As their names imply, these are slender, graceful, fast-moving snakes. Long, thin tails, large eyes, and a restless, aggressive disposition are shared by all the species in these groups. Whether they occur in America, Europe, Asia, or Africa, the racers have similar habits and diet, which may range from small rodents to frogs and other snakes. Many live in hot, dry climates and even along the borders of deserts, as in Algeria. The attractive horseshoe snake is one of these racers inhabiting the north coast of Africa, although it also occurs in southeastern Europe.

One of the most common of all North American racers is the familiar blacksnake, or black racer (not to be confused with the pilot blacksnake, the heavier bodied black rat snake described earlier). Its maximum length is six feet, but few black racers exceed a length of four feet. Because they lack the powers of constriction, racers have to be content with small prey, and confine themselves to such animals as mice, frogs, and small birds.

Reports about the speed of these snakes have been exaggerated, although the coachwhip snake, fastest of all the racers, can move so rapidly that a man on foot can barely overtake it. Excessively long and thin, the whip snakes are so gracefully agile in movement that it is very difficult to keep up with them on rough terrain, where they can slip through bushes and around obstacles with a speed that may appear incredible to a pursuer.

The longest colubrid snake of the Old World is also a racer, a Burmese species that may grow to a length of twelve feet. Another Asian species, a very slender, whiplike snake with a nervous disposition, is only slightly smaller, with a

The handsome indigo snake is the largest nonvenomous snake of North America.

maximum length of ten feet. Its name, "greater Indian rat snake," is confusing because it is not closely related to the rat snakes, even though it likes to feed on rodents. For that reason these snakes are economically important and deserve all the protection they can get.

The largest and most heavy-bodied of the New World racers are members of a small tropical genus. One, called the indigo snake, occurs in the most southerly parts of the United States. It is a handsome, gleaming blue-black species that may attain a length of eight feet, although most individuals are much smaller. Despite its relatively heavy body, it is a fast, agile animal that has the habits of the typical racer. Similar species occur in Central and South America.

The slenderest of all snakes are a group found in the tropics of both the Old and New Worlds. Ranging in length from two to five feet, even the longest are so thin that they look like vines. Known as tropical whip, or tree, snakes, these large-eyed, dainty creatures are gorgeously colored in metallic green, bronze, and gold hues. Their delicate beauty has won them admirers even among people who normally dislike snakes.

Although the majority of nonvenomous snakes can be grouped in the preceding categories, there are a number of smaller groups containing interesting members. The North American hog-nosed snakes, for instance, are famed for their convincing mimicry of poisonous snakes, a performance that often costs them their life when people mistake them for a venomous species.

Many snakes, of course, try to bluff when molested: a number of harmless species hiss, vibrate their tail tips, or flatten their heads and necks and weave from side to side in an attempt to appear threatening. The hog-nosed snake, however, puts on a performance that should get it a prize as the best actor of snakedom. When one of these snakes is molested, it flattens its neck and at the same time emits a series of long and loud hisses. It may even pretend to strike like a venomous snake when an intruder comes too close, hoping to scare him off in this way. However, if that does not happen, the hog-nosed snake quickly drops its threatening attitude and suddenly seems to be overcome by convulsions. Twisting and

The ring-necked snake, with its tail coiled to appear threatening.

writing, the little faker flops over on its back, where it lies
with gaping mouth, limp and motionless and apparently quite
dead. If it is righted at this stage, it immediately flops over

A hog-nosed snake playing dead.

again on its back, a position it apparently considers necessary for a convincing performance. If the intruder waits patiently nearby without further disturbing the "dead" snake, he soon sees it miraculously returning to life: first the hog-nose cautiously lifts its head for a quick look around to survey the situation; then if the coast seems clear, it turns over on its belly and slithers away as fast as possible.

Actually, the hog-nosed snake is probably one of the most inoffensive of all nonvenomous snakes. It owes its name to a nose turned up like a wedge, a useful tool for burrowing in search of toads, which make up the main part of its diet. Unfortunately, the acting talents of this harmless snake, which

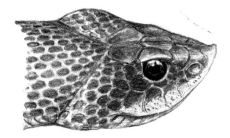

The head of a hog-nosed snake.

hardly ever can be induced to bite, have given it an evil reputation, a fact borne out by such local names as puff adder, blow adder, and hissing adder. Thousands are killed because people mistake this gentle creature, frequently found in sandy areas, including coastal regions, for a dangerous venomous species.

There are two other North American snakes that are the subjects—and sometimes the victims—of erroneous but persistent stories about their alleged habits. Both the rainbow mud snake and the red-bellied mud snake occur in the southern-most parts of the United States. Secretive types that like to burrow and hide in damp soil, these two large—up to six feet long—and brilliantly colored snakes have given rise to sensational tales, as indicated by their local names of hoop snake and stinging snake. According to these stories, a snake of this type can take its tail in its mouth, draw itself up into a vertical hooplike position, stiffen its body, and then rapidly roll away. As if this were not enough, the snake is also supposed to be capable of delivering a dangerous, scorpion-like sting with the tip of its tail.

As usual, there is some basis for both stories, even though the facts have become embellished beyond recognition. Both snakes have the habit of lying in a coiled position in which the head may rest close to the tail, thus forming an almost

The rainbow mud snake, lying in a coiled position.

perfect circle. Even zoologists have occasionally mistaken one of these snakes for an old bicycle tire thrown into a ditch. That is the extent of the factual basis for the hoop snake theory. The stinging tail is closer to the truth, for the tail of both snakes ends in a scale as sharp as a spine. When the snake is captured, it presses this needle-like spiny tip against its captor's arm or hand in an effort to frighten him and free itself. This often works; the surprise of the unexpected needle prick, which may draw a drop of blood, frequently causes the captor to drop the snake, which then can manage to escape.

Other harmless snakes with unusual anatomical features are the chunk- or blunt-headed snakes of Asia and South America, in which the neck may taper to the circumference of a match, making the head appear incongruously large. The excessively thin neck prevents these snakes from swallowing any except very small prey, such as slugs, worms, and insects.

The prize for ugliness among snakes would probably go to the river snakes. Almost all are found in Asia. The karung, or elephant-trunk snake, occurs especially in Malaysia and is representative of the entire group. A thick-set, brownish animal, the snake appears extremely sluggish and stupid. Captive elephant-trunk snakes were observed to remain underwater much of the time. These reptiles have evidently developed a way of extracting some oxygen from the water, enabling them to stay below the surface for long periods. Although this snake occurs widely in Malaysia, it may soon be exterminated through ruthless slaughter for its valuable hide, which is much sought after because it makes fine leather for shoes and pocketbooks.

One of the most highly specialized of all snakes is the egg-eating snake of tropical and South Africa. This small, yellowish-olive or light brown snake, which rarely exceeds a length

An egg-eating snake swallowing an egg.

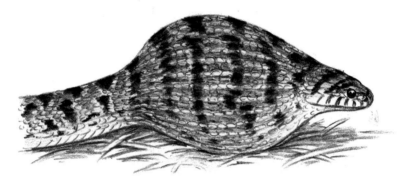

The split-open shell will soon be crushed by constriction of the snake's neck muscles.

of two feet, lives exclusively on birds' eggs and has a unique apparatus for dealing with the hard shells. Although many other snakes like to vary their diet with eggs, they either wait for gastric juices to dissolve the shell or break it by muscular contraction; in either case, the shell is swallowed by the snake along with its contents. The egg-eating snake employs a different method. It has no teeth in its jaws, and it does not need them, for it does not have to secure struggling prey. Instead, it has "teeth" of a sort in its throat—sawlike projections of the neck vertebrae that extend into the throat. As the egg is swallowed, this "egg saw" cuts the shell and releases the contents into the stomach. Contractions of the throat muscles then squeeze the egg-shell fragments into a compact mass, which is regurgitated. One captive egg-eating snake survived nicely on a diet of about ten or twelve pigeons' eggs per month.

It is easy to see from this limited review of the harmless snakes of the world that these reptiles have successfully made use of every environmental niche, from aquatic habitats and underground burrows to life in the treetops. More evidence that the loss of limbs has not kept any snake from earning a highly successful living appears in the chapters that follow.

Rear-Fanged Snakes

Rear-fanged snakes constitute an intermediate category between the nonvenomous and the dangerously poisonous species. Although the rear-fanged snakes possess a venom, in most cases it has very low toxicity and usually does not affect human beings. The venom-conducting fangs, which are located in the rear of the upper jaw—hence the collective name—are of a primitive structure.

Equipped with merely an open groove for the flow of venom, the fangs are comparatively inefficient for delivering the poison into the victim's bloodstream to benumb or paralyze it. In addition most of these snakes are not very large and generally have a mild-tempered disposition. They do not strike at an intruder, so that the fangs can become embedded only if the snake bites and then gets a firm hold in a manner usually reserved for prey only. However, some of the largest members are potentially dangerous and are treated with caution by the experts. Although reports of human fatalities

from bites of rear-fanged snakes have not been reliably sub-
stantiated, enough people have become gravely ill as a result
of such bites to warrant extreme caution. By and large, however, the record of these mostly medium-sized and nonag-
gressive snakes is clean. Their original scientific name was
Suspecta, but the classification has long since been changed;
they are now considered a subfamily of the colubrid snakes.

The majority of rear-fanged snakes feed on cold-blooded
prey, such as lizards, frogs, and other snakes, while the
smaller species confine themselves to a diet of insects and
worms. Only a few species prey upon warm-blooded animals,
mostly small birds; their venom is comparatively more toxic
—sufficiently strong to paralyze and even kill a bird quickly.

That rear-fanged snakes are generally mild-tempered is
illustrated by one of the largest species, the mussarana, which
may reach a length of eight feet. Despite its wide range that
extends from Guatemala to Brazil, the mussarana is not a
common snake. Captives have proved to be gentle; reportedly
even large ones do not bite when handled. This is astonishing
because the mussarana is a fearless hunter and killer of other
snakes, including some of the most dangerously venomous
species of those regions. In attacking such poisonous snakes as
the deadly fer-de-lance pit viper, the mussarana employs constriction and at the same time tries to embed its fangs in an
effort to inject the benumbing poison into the viper. With prey
of that kind, however, the weak venom is not very effective,
and it is mainly the power of its muscles that eventually en-
ables the mussarana to overcome its victim. Although the
viper often succeeds in sinking its own large poison fangs deep
into the body of its enemy, the mussarana, like most snake-
eating species, seems quite immune to the virulent venom.

Evidently the only rear-fanged snake dangerous to man is

The African boomslang, a rear-fanged snake with potent venom.

the South African boomslang, a Dutch name meaning tree snake. This five-foot, grayish-green arboreal snake differs from most other rear-fanged snakes in its preference for warm-blooded prey—chiefly birds. Normally a mild-tempered species, it tends to be more irritable than other rear-fanged species and may bite savagely if molested or cornered. Several human fatalities have been attributed to this snake by the settlers of the region, and it is generally feared. Even though there seems to be no conclusive proof of a person dying from the bite of this bush dweller, its venom appears to affect both the blood and the nerves, and great caution in handling the boomslang is indicated.

The thin-bodied vine snake of the Southwest is one of the few North American rear-fanged species.

Another large, handsome rear-fanged snake, treated with respect because of its size, is the Malaysian mangrove snake (see illustration on page 74). Patterned in glistening black with bright yellow rings spaced at intervals, it looks like an artificial object made of shiny plastic as long as it remains motionless. A mild-mannered species, it seems loath to bite even when handled. It grows to a length of six feet, and has comparatively large fangs. Like the boomslang, it feeds largely on birds, which its venom quickly overcomes.

Many instances of parallel evolutionary development are found among rear-fanged snakes; certain species have evolved characteristics similar to those of nonvenomous groups without being closely related. There are, for example, the extremely thin, usually green or brown, arboreal species of South

America, known popularly as vine snakes. One pretty species is the green whip snake (not to be confused with nonvenomous whip snakes) of Central America. Although it may grow to a length of four feet, it is so thin that the body at its thickest part is a scant half inch in diameter. Its head is very elongated, and its tail looks like a piece of thin string. Colored a light leaf green with a lemon-yellow stripe on each side, this snake is difficult to distinguish from the stems and vines of the bushes it inhabits. The prey of these dainty snakes consists mostly of small arboreal lizards. One vine snake found in the extreme southwestern parts of the United States is brown with white along the sides.

Similar kinds of slender rear-fanged arboreal snakes occur in Asia. One of the oddest is the long-nosed tree snake, which

A South American vine snake.

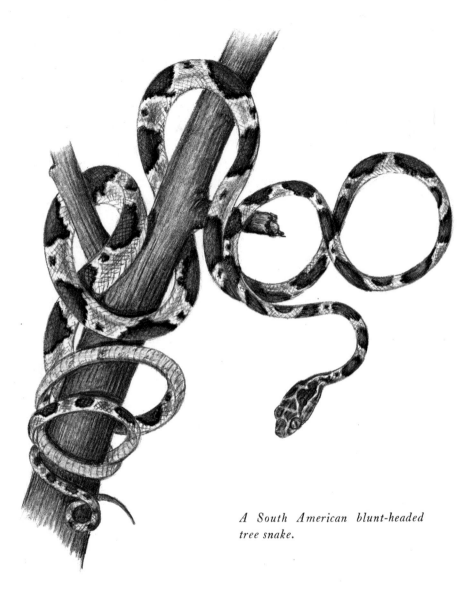

A South American blunt-headed tree snake.

deserves its name, for its nose is long and pointed like the tip of a sharpened pencil. Everything else about this snake is also elongate: although it may reach a length of five feet, its body and tail are as thin as those of the South American kinds, and even the pupils of its eyes are horizontal slits.

Other groups with characteristics similar to those of non-venomous species are the Indian and Indo-Chinese water or river snakes, docile, rather ugly creatures that feed on fish and frogs; and the so-called night snakes, nocturnal species also known as cat-eyed snakes because of their elliptical pupils. The thin, tapering necks and comparatively broad, blunt heads of these snakes make them look very much like the non-venomous chunk-headed snakes described in the preceding chapter. The blunt-headed tree snake of South America is a typical representative of this group. This species and its relatives have the peculiar habit of strongly compressing the body laterally so that it resembles an I-beam. This makes the body much more rigid, which is of considerable help when the snake wants to span the distance between two branches.

Perhaps the most striking case of parallel development is the rear-fanged egg-eating snake of India, which has an "egg-saw" in its throat similar to that of its nonvenomous counterpart in Africa. Since both the venom and the poison fangs are quite useless to this egg-eating species, it would seem reasonable to assume that these features will be lost during future evolutionary development.

The most colorful of all the rear-fanged snakes are the various small, inoffensive species of Central and South America that appear to imitate the highly venomous, brilliantly red-yellow-and-black-banded coral snakes of those regions. Some naturalists believe that the harmless imitators may reap a certain advantage by looking so much like the dangerous true coral snakes, but that theory has not been proved and is open to argument.

Rear-fanged snakes include one group, the so-called flying snakes, that has evolved what ranks as perhaps the most peculiar specialization in the entire snake world. These reptiles are

A so-called flying snake.

found in Southeast Asia, especially in Burma and on the islands of Sumatra, Borneo, and Java. Rather small and stout snakes that rarely attain a length of three feet, they prey on the arboreal lizards of those regions. If such a snake has crawled out on a limb and wants to get somewhere else quickly, it launches itself into the air and glides down to the bush or branch it wants to reach. By flattening the body and extending the ribs sideways, the snakes turn themselves into somewhat concave soaring planes. Since they cannot really fly or propel themselves in any direction but downward, "gliding snake" would be a much more appropriate name for these reptiles. All the same, it is an interesting and unusual specialization for reptiles with cylindrical bodies.

After having reviewed the species that represent an evolutionary bridge between the nonvenomous and dangerously poisonous snakes, we are ready to take a look at the most advanced and at the same time most feared members of the entire group.

How to Keep a Pet Snake

Snakes and other reptiles have recently become fashionable pets. Unfortunately, lack of knowledge about the requirements of these animals in captivity often leads to their premature death through starvation or illness. Yet it is usually quite simple to provide an environment in which local species can survive and remain healthy and content. Exotic reptiles present a much more difficult problem and may need expert attention.

Before deciding to keep a snake as a pet, you should consider the following questions:

1. Can you provide suitable and adequate living quarters for the animal? Figure that a snake fifteen inches long needs at least a cubic foot of living space.

2. Can you provide the necessary food? Small snakes are easy to feed, but larger species feed on live animals, such as mice, rats, and frogs, and this becomes a difficult and often unpleasant and messy problem.

3. Can—and will—you take the time and patience necessary to clean the cage periodically? Like all animals confined in a limited space, the snake needs clean quarters to stay healthy.

4. Is there any strenuous objection to your pet in your family? Many people are afraid of snakes and find them repulsive. If there is such a person in your family and your pet escapes from its cage some day, it could lead to a somewhat disagreeable situation.

If you can answer all of these questions satisfactorily, it is time to select the snake you want so that you can prepare its cage. The keeping of venomous snakes is not recommended for the amateur. In North America there are a number of small- to medium-sized nonvenomous snakes that make fine pets. First and foremost are the garter snakes, which are common throughout the United States and the southern parts of Canada. They rarely exceed a length of three feet; the related ribbon snake is very slender and more delicate. Either the rough or the smooth green snake makes a fine pet if it can be induced to take food. A number of attractive small snakes about fifteen inches in length include the pretty ring-necked snakes and the brown snakes. The latter are quite common but rarely seen because of their secretive habits.

The small red-bellied snake makes an attractive pet.

The rough-scaled green snake.

Larger snakes that make good pets are the rosy boa, the corn snake, the fox snake, and the milk, or red king, snake. The hog-nosed snake also makes an interesting pet, although it usually stops its dramatic play-acting (described on page 67) as soon as it gets tame.

The cage for a snake has to be prepared not only according to its size, but also with consideration for its living habits.

Garter snakes, for example, are related to the water snakes, and some, like the ribbon snake, are more or less aquatic. A basin with water, large enough for the snake to submerge in, must be supplied for such species. Green snakes, on the other hand, are partially arboreal; they feel most comfortable if some leafy plants and branches are placed in their cage. The difficulty of keeping fresh plants in the cage can be overcome by using a stout branch and decorating it with artificial leaves. Almost all snakes like to hide occasionally, and some species, such as DeKay's snake, spend a large part of their lives hidden away in crevices or under stones. They will not stay healthy long if deprived of such hiding places in the terrarium as a curved piece of bark or a flat stone placed over a hollowed-out depression in one corner of the cage.

The basic preparation of the terrarium that will house your snake is simple. You can use an old aquarium or a large

A diagram showing the various layers of a well-balanced terrarium.

box made of clear plastic. Cover the bottom with coarse gravel and a few pieces of charcoal. Then add a layer of fine gravel, and finally some sand, firmly packed, over half of the area. The other half should be covered with potting soil or humus. Into the soil place a shallow water basin large enough to accommodate the coiled-up snake if it is a more or less aquatic species. The ribbon snake, for example, likes to take its food from the water. Partially arboreal snakes, such as the green snake, can live with just a small water container.

The portion of the terrarium covered with soil may be planted with some moss and a few small plants. A large stone or piece of bark can be used to fashion a convenient hiding place, and a short branch decorated with artificial leaves will provide something for the snake to climb on.

A tight-fitting lid made of a wooden frame and wire mesh is the best cover for the terrarium. Most snakes have surprising strength and can push the lid up unless it fits snugly.

Many reptiles suffer from mineral and vitamin deficiencies when in captivity because their food is usually much more monotonous than the diet they get in the wild. To overcome the deficiencies, a small piece of one of the mineral-vitamin preparations sold for keeping fish healthy in aquaria may be placed in the water dish of your snake.

Most snakes need to be fed a good meal only once a week; feeding them once every three days is more than adequate. A well-fed, healthy snake can survive a fast of several weeks, if necessary, without ill effects.

The type of food depends upon the species. Both the rough and the smooth green snakes like insects, especially caterpillars, grasshoppers, beetles, and grubs. Make sure that the insects you select as food for your snake are not species that deserve protection. For example, the caterpillars of the cabbage butterfly, most moths, Japanese beetles, the so-called wire worms, and other destructive insects are good and proper food for your snakes. Caterpillars of swallowtails and other rare, beautiful butterflies, as well as such beneficial insects as flower flies and their aphid-devouring grubs, should never be fed to snakes. In the winter mealworms are the easiest food to obtain, but in the summer the diet should be as varied as possible.

Garter snakes can usually be fed earthworms; mixing raw hamburger with the earthworms may induce your snake eventually to accept bits of meat. Ribbon snakes are fish eaters, and in the beginning you may have to feed them small live fish or tadpoles; later, thin strips of fish (frozen fish has to be defrosted first) may be tied loosely to a piece of string and moved in the water to simulate a live fish. Once the snake gets used to eating such pieces, your feeding problems are all but over. Your pet may even become tame enough to take the fish from your fingers.

The very small snakes—DeKay's, red-bellied, and ring-necked—feed on small insects and worms, including tubifex worms, small earthworms, and grubs. They also take mealworms, although they generally prefer the more soft-bodied grubs.

The larger snakes require live mice or young rats. Many will also accept eggs occasionally; the corn and fox snakes and other members of the rat-snake group especially are fond of eggs.

Small snakes should not be handled much; they do not tolerate it well. Snakes over thirty inches long can stand more handling, but even then it should be kept at a minimum.

The cage should never be placed so that the snake cannot escape direct sunlight if it wishes to do so. In the winter, a lamp with an incandescent bulb should provide light and warmth several hours a day.

If your pet snake has a sufficiently large and clean cage, proper food and water, and is not handled excessively, you should be able to keep it healthy, and perhaps, in time, it will become tame enough to climb on your hand without hesitation. If you make a hobby of observing it closely, you may even discover a heretofore unknown fact about the species to which it belongs, for much about the habits of even the common snakes is still to be discovered.

Ranges of Familiar
North American Snakes

Blacksnake, common, see *Racer, black.*

Blacksnake, pilot, also called black chicken snake or mountain blacksnake (see ills. pp. 39 and 62). From Florida to central Massachusetts, west to Texas.

Boa, rosy (see ill. p. 50). Mexico and southern California.

Boa, rubber (see ill. p. 50). Pacific coast region, from lower California to Washington.

Brown snakes, see *DeKay's snake, Red-bellied snake.*

Bull snake, common. Mississippi Valley to Rocky Mountains. Closely related species occur in the West (gopher snake) and in the East (see *Pine snake*).

Chicken snake, see *Rat snake, Blacksnake, pilot.*

Coachwhip snake (see ill. p. 64). Virginia to Florida, west to the Rockies. Similar species inhabit the Southwest.

Copperhead, also called highland moccasin (see ill. p. 102). Central Massachusetts to northern Florida, west to Illinois and Texas.

Copperhead

Water moccasin \\\

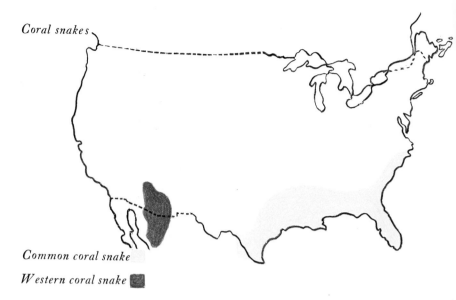

Coral snakes

Common coral snake

Western coral snake ▨

Coral snake, common (see ill. p. 88). South Carolina and Mississippi to Florida, the Gulf States, and Mexico.

Coral snake, western or *sonoran* (see ill. p. 88). Southern New Mexico, Arizona, and northern Mexico.

Corn snake (see ill. p. 54). Southern New Jersey to Florida and westward to the Mississippi.

Cottonmouth, see *Water moccasin.*

DeKay's snake (see ill. p. 58). Entire eastern half of the United States and southern Canada.

Fox snake. Indiana, Iowa, Michigan, Minnesota.

Garter snake, common (see ill. p. 58). Florida to Canada, west to Minnesota. Similar species and subspecies occur in almost every part of the United States.

Glossy snake. Southwestern United States and Mexico.

Gopher snake, see *Indigo snake, Bull snake, common.*

Green snake, smooth. From Florida to southern Canada, west to New Mexico.

Green snake, rough-scaled (see ill. p. 111). Southern United States, north to New Jersey.

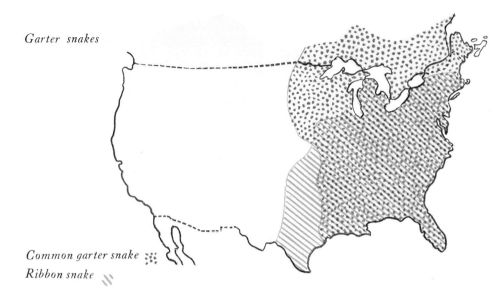

Garter snakes

Common garter snake :::
Ribbon snake \\\

Hog-nosed snake, common (see ills. pp. 68, 69). Massachusetts to Florida,
 west to the Mississippi Valley. Similar species are found in other parts
 of the United States.

Indigo snake (see ill. p. 66). Florida and southeastern United States.

King snake, California (see ill. p. 60). California.

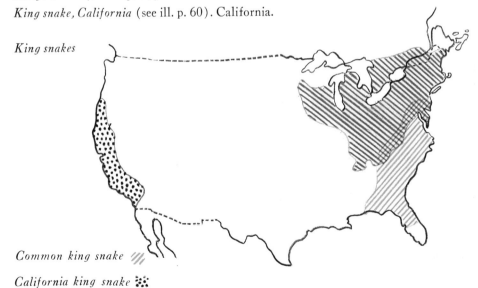

King snakes

Common king snake ///
California king snake :::
Red king snake \\\

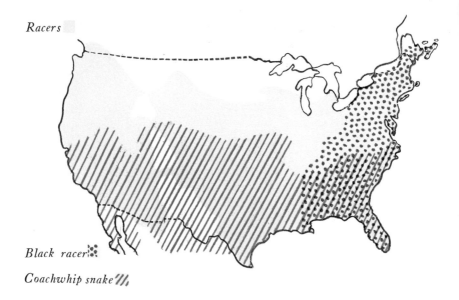

Racers

Black racer

Coachwhip snake

King snake, common (see ill. p. 60). Southern New Jersey to Florida.

King snake, scarlet (see ill. p. 60). Mountainous regions of California and Arizona.

Massasauga. Western New York through Ohio to Nebraska, north to Michigan, south to Texas.

Mud snake, also called horn snake. Louisiana, the Mississippi Valley, and Indiana.

Mud snake, rainbow (see ill. p. 70). Southern Virginia to Florida, west to Alabama.

Pine snake (see ill. p. 63). Southern New Jersey to Florida and Gulf States.

Racer, black, or *common blacksnake*. Entire eastern part of the United States.

Racer, blue (see ill. p. 64). Central and southwestern United States. Similar species are found in the West.

Rat snake, black, see *Blacksnake, pilot*.

Rat snake, gray. Gulf States region.

Rat snake, yellow, also called yellow chicken snake or yellow house snake. New Jersey to Florida, west to the Mississippi.

Rat snakes

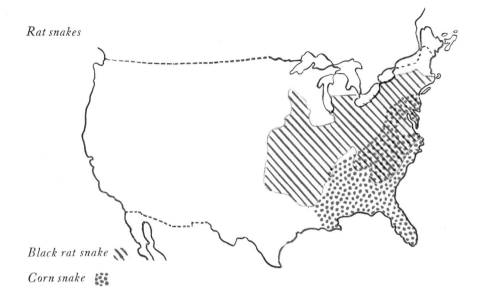

Black rat snake

Corn snake

Rattlesnake, timber (see ill. p. 104). Maine to Great Plains, Florida, Arkansas, and eastern Texas.
Rattlesnake, western diamondback. Texas, New Mexico, Arizona, and California.

Rattlesnakes

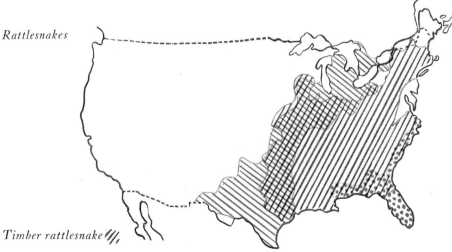

Timber rattlesnake

Massasauga

Eastern diamondback

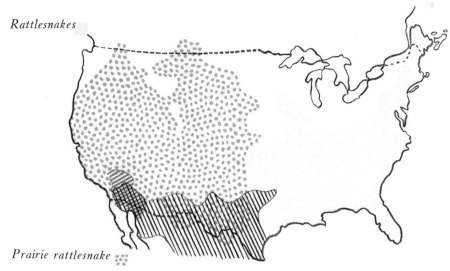

Rattlesnakes

Prairie rattlesnake

Sidewinder

Red diamond rattlesnake

Rattlesnake, eastern diamondback (see ill. p. 104). Coastal areas of south-eastern United States.

Rattlesnake, horned, see *Sidewinder.*

Rattlesnake, pigmy. From North Carolina to Florida, west to Texas.

Rattlesnake, prairie. Great Plains from eastern Nebraska to Rocky Mountains, south to central Texas and Mexico.

Rattlesnake, red diamond (see ill. p. 106). Southern California and Mexico.

Red-bellied snake (see ill. p. 110). Ontario to southern Mexico, west to Kansas.

Ribbon snake. Southeastern Canada to the Mississippi Valley and Georgia.

Ring-necked snake, eastern (see ill. p. 67). Southern Canada to Florida, west to Illinois. Similar species are found in the West.

Scarlet snake (see ill. p. 108). Southeastern parts of the United States.

Sidewinder. Southern California, Nevada, Arizona.

Vine snake (see ill. p. 78). Extreme southwestern region of the United States.

Water moccasin. Virginia to Florida and the Gulf States into eastern Texas.

Water snake, common. Southern Canada to Florida and west to the Mississippi Valley. Similar species are found, along with the common kind, in various parts of the same area.

Water snakes and *Brown snakes*

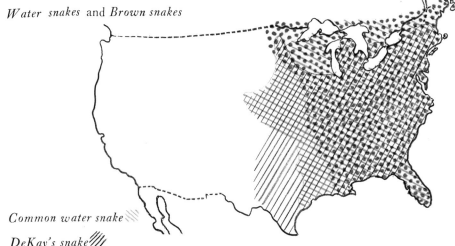

Common water snake

DeKay's snake

Red-bellied snake

Index

(Page numbers in italics refer to illustrations.)